BECOMING

WHO WE ARE

A STUDY OF EPHESIANS

Unless otherwise noted, Scripture quotations have been taken from the Holy Bible, New International Version®, NIV® Copyright © 1973, 1978, 1984, 2011 by Biblica, Inc.® Used by permission. All rights reserved worldwide.

ISBN 978-1-7351518-2-3

Freshwater Publications
Freshwater Church
138 West First Street
Waconia, Minnesota 55387

CONTENTS

About This Study

WELCOME

At Freshwater, we are committed to helping people grow in their faith. Ultimately, it is our prayer that you fall deeper in love with Jesus and His Word through the power of the Holy Spirit every day. This Bible study workbook is a tool to be used by you - individually or in a group – to grow in your faith.

BECOMING WHO WE ARE

"[4] But because of his great love for us, God, who is rich in mercy, [5] made us alive with Christ even when we were dead in transgressions... [8] For it is by grace you have been saved, through faith—and this is not from yourselves, it is the gift of God— [9] not by works, so that no one can boast. [10] For we are God's handiwork, created in Christ Jesus to do good works, which God prepared in advance for us to do."

Ephesians 2:4-5,8-10

The beautiful reality of the gospel message is that we were dead in our sin, and Christ made us alive! He brought us new life in Him, not because we earned it but because of His love and mercy. We were dead but now we are spiritually alive. We are the children of God – we are no longer who we were.

However, we still find ourselves in our sinful flesh surrounded by a broken world. God's work of transforming us and working through us for His good plans, is a process.

It's a process of becoming who we are.

The Book of Ephesians

Paul's Letter to the Church in Ephesus

Most credible scholars agree that the Apostle Paul authored the letter to the Ephesians. Not only is this stated in the first verse of the chapter, but the letter itself reflects similar grammatical structure with the other letters he authored under the inspiration of the Holy Spirit.

Paul's letter to the Ephesians is considered to be one of the prison epistles. Epistle is a literary work in the form of a letter. The prison epistles are so named because they were written by the Apostle Paul while he was under house arrest in Rome. There are four prison epistles: Ephesians, Philippians, Colossians, and Philemon.

The exact date of his incarceration is unknown, but scholars believe it was between AD 60-62. Paul's imprisonment is mentioned in the book of Acts. We do know he was guarded by soldiers (Acts 28:16), permitted to receive visitors (Acts 28:30), and had the opportunity to share the gospel (Acts 28:31). He did not have these opportunities during his two-year imprisonment in Caesarea.

Paul's letter to the Ephesians reflects Paul's concerns for believers. The first half of the book teaches the truth of the gospel message and who we are now in Christ. The second half includes instructions on the practical application of it.

HISTORY & BACKGROUND OF THE CITY OF EPHESUS

At the time the city of Ephesus was the seacoast capital of proconsular Asia. The city was one of Asia's most prominent cities because of its political influence, commercial businesses, and grand religious center. Ephesus was home to a massive temple dedicated to the goddess "Artemis." This temple took over 200 years to build and is still considered to be one of the seven wonders of the ancient world.

THE CONFLICT IN EPHESUS

Because Ephesus was such a significant religious center many silver images of demon gods were made and sold for large profits. Magical arts were commonplace and even the Jews had erected a synagogue in town (Acts 18:19, 19:8).

When Paul went throughout Asia teaching against idol worship, he faced opposition from the professional metal workers who made silver images of the goddess Artemis. Since they sold them for a profit, they saw Paul as a threat to their livelihood. They were more concerned about making money than worshiping their goodness Artemis (Acts 19:24-41). The leader of the metalworkers was Demetrius, and he incited all the other silversmiths to oppose Paul. This resulted in a riot where Paul's companions, Gaius and Aristarchus, were dragged to the public theater.

ILLUSTRATIONS

Paul uses common illustrations to point out deeper spiritual truths just like Jesus. Jesus often used fishing illustrations like when He said to Peter "follow Me and I'll make you a fisher of men." He spoke of Himself as our Shepherd and His followers as His sheep. One of the most well-known and powerful illustrations in scripture comes from Paul's description of putting on the armor of God in chapter six. In all probability, Paul was chained to a Roman guard when God inspired Paul to use this powerful example illustrating spiritual truth.

CONCLUSION

Paul's challenge to the Ephesians was to live differently because they have been called by Christ. Through fierce opposition from depraved people and demonic spiritual powers, many people came to faith in Christ and the gospel took root and grew, Acts 19 records this:

"Many of those who believed now came and openly confessed what they had done. A number who had practiced sorcery brought their scrolls together and burned them publicly. When they calculated the value of the scrolls, the total came to fifty thousand drachmas. In this way the word of the Lord spread widely and grew in power."

Acts 19:18-20

The apostle Paul's influence made a significant difference in the lives of the believers in Ephesus and shaped how they lived out their faith in the spiritually bankrupt city. Paul speaks to the timeless doctrinal and practical issues facing every Christian encouraging them to live a Christ-centered life. The same wisdom that Paul shared with the Ephesians under the inspiration of the Holy Spirit still applies to believers today.

CHOSEN
Ephesians 1:1-14

BIBLE READING

- **Sunday:** Ephesians 1:1-14
- **Monday:** 2 Corinthians 1:20-24
- **Tuesday:** Colossians 1:12-14
- **Wednesday:** 1 Peter 1:3-5
- **Thursday:** Romans 8:15-17
- **Friday:** Galatians 3:26-29
- **Saturday:** Titus 3:4-7

OPENING DISCUSSION

1. Describe a time when someone was picked or was chosen first for something special (award, team, privilege of some kind, etc.). How do you think that made them feel?

2. Do you think people have a desire to feel needed or chosen for a purpose? Why or why not?

STUDY SUMMARY

We are chosen by God. We are chosen to receive redemption through Jesus Christ. We are chosen to be united under the banner of Christ. We have been given the Holy Spirit as a seal–guaranteeing our inheritance as chosen children of God.

DISCUSSION

Read Ephesians 1:1-14, then answer the following questions.

1. According to Paul, when were we chosen by God? Why do you think that is important?

2. Looking at verses 4-6; what were we chosen for?

3. What does it mean to be "predestined"?

4. Looking at verses 7-8; what is Jesus' role in salvation? What is our role?

5. What is the mystery that has now been made known?

6. What is the purpose of this mystery? How do we, as followers of Jesus, promote unity in our culture today?

7. According to Paul, what is the mark of belief?

8. What is the Holy Spirit guaranteeing for us?

FOOD FOR THOUGHT

"God the Father planned the church, God the Son paid for the church, and God the Holy Spirit protects the church. The source of all our blessings is the God and Father of our Lord Jesus Christ. He carries our mind back to eternity past to make us realize that salvation is altogether of God and not at all of ourselves."

-Thru The Bible with J. Vernon McGee[1]

APPLICATION

Oftentimes we don't feel loved, or we feel unworthy because of something we have done or said. Remember, we all make mistakes, but God still loves you! You are His child, adopted into his family for His purpose. In the same way that a good parent lavishes love upon their child, God lavishes His love on you.

So, this week live with the understanding that you are a child of God, your sins are forgiven, and that He has plans and a purpose for you.

PRAYER POINTS

- Give thanks to God for 3 things He has done for you.

- Pray for an increase of wisdom and understanding of His Word.

- Pray for the empowering filling of the Holy Spirit in your life and His leading.

STUDY ON YOUR OWN

1. Read John 17:20-26. What does Jesus' prayer teach us about who we are and how we are called to live?

2. Do a word study on "mystery" in the New Testament by reading the passages listed below. Pay special attention to what the "mystery" is, how it has been revealed, and what we are called to do with the "mystery" that has been revealed.

   - Romans 16:25-26

   - 1 Corinthians 2:6-10

   - Colossians 1:24-29

3. Memorize Ephesians 1:4-5. To help in memorizing it, write it out several times here:

NOTES

KNOW THE HOPE
Ephesians 1:15-23

BIBLE READING

- **Sunday:** Ephesians 1:15-23
- **Monday:** Colossians 1:9-12
- **Tuesday:** Philippians 1:9-11
- **Wednesday:** 1 Corinthians 2:10-16
- **Thursday:** James 1:2-5
- **Friday:** John 14:16-17
- **Saturday:** 2 Timothy 1:7

OPENING DISCUSSION

1. What are some common challenges or distractions in your daily life?

2. How do you currently experience and express your hope in Christ?

STUDY SUMMARY

Paul's prayer for the Ephesians, and for us, is that we continue to grow in our understanding of our chosen status. In order to do so, there must be a deepening of our spiritual understanding (our heads) and a deepening of our affection (our hearts). In Christ, we have a great, living hope. Life's difficulties and busyness cause us to forget this hope. Paul's reminder is for believers to always know the hope we have in Christ.

DISCUSSION

Read Ephesians 1:15-23, then answer the following questions.

1. Paul expresses gratitude for the Ephesians' faith and love. Remember Paul wrote this while in prison. How does Paul's gratitude for their spiritual growth challenge or inspire your own faith journey?

2. According to verses 16-18, what three things does Paul do/ask for the believers when he prays for them?

3. From verse 18 - What is it that the "eyes of your heart" are meant to see? Why do you think these three realities are so crucial for us to grasp?

4. Paul prays for the Ephesians to have a deeper understanding of their hope in Christ. What are some practical ways you can deepen your own spiritual understanding and experience of this hope?

5. How do life's difficulties and busy schedules affect your ability to maintain focus on your hope in Christ? What strategies have you found helpful in keeping this hope alive amidst challenges?

6. In what ways can a deepened affection for Christ impact your relationships with others? How does this affection shape your actions and attitudes toward those around you?

7. Verse 19 speaks of a 'incomparably great power" - What is this power? And why does Paul include it here?

8. How can understanding the 'hope of His calling' help us respond to feelings of doubt or insecurity about our future? What role does this hope play in shaping your outlook on life's uncertainties?

9. Paul's prayer is for believers to have both spiritual understanding and affection. How can this group support each other in growing both in knowledge and affection in our faith?

FOOD FOR THOUGHT

"In Ephesians 1:15-23, Paul's prayer is not for the Ephesians to receive more gifts or blessings, but to grasp what they have already been given. The emphasis is on a deeper spiritual insight into the reality of their chosen status, the immense power of God in their lives, and the hope of their calling. This passage underscores that the Christian life is not about achieving new spiritual heights, but about awakening to the profound truths that are already ours in Christ. It is a call to recognize and live out the extraordinary hope, power, and inheritance we possess through Jesus, which radically transforms our perception of our daily struggles and our place in God's grand design."

-Timothy Keller[2]

APPLICATION

To apply the insights of this week's study, we need to embrace the profound spiritual truth already available to us in Christ. Instead of seeking a new experience, focus on deepening your understanding of what you already have in Christ - you are a chosen child with an inheritance and hope.

This week spend time reflecting on what you already have in Christ. In your own words, describe your hope in Christ:

PRAYER POINTS

- Pray for deeper understanding of God's Word and affection for Jesus.

- Pray for focus and wisdom for when to say "no" to the busyness of life.

- Pray for 2 other people that you can share the hope you've found in Christ.

STUDY ON YOUR OWN

1. Reflect on a specific challenge you are currently experiencing and consider how the spiritual truth of Ephesians 1:15-23 might influence your approach to it.

2. Identify specific spiritual practices or habits that you could incorporate into your routine to enhance your understanding and experience of the truth of God's Word.

3.   Memorize Colossians 1:27. To help in memorizing it, write it out several
     times here:

NOTES

BIBLE READING

- **Sunday:** Ephesians 2:1-10
- **Monday:** Romans 5:6-11
- **Tuesday:** Titus 3:3-7
- **Wednesday:** 1 Peter 2:9-10
- **Thursday:** John 3:16-18
- **Friday:** 2 Corinthians 5:17-21
- **Saturday:** Acts 15:7-11

OPENING DISCUSSION

1. Describe a time in your life when you felt like you just could not measure up no matter how hard you tried.

2. Have you ever received an unexpected or undeserved gift? How did it make you feel? Was it hard to receive? Why?

STUDY SUMMARY

In today's section of text, the Apostle Paul boldly clarifies a profound spiritual truth. Left to ourselves, there is nothing but death and destruction in our future. Selfish desires rule our hearts, and we are deserving of the coming punishment.

Yet, God offers us life, an opportunity to really live. Despite our natural inclination to sin, everyone has been given the opportunity to live a new life in Christ. Paul assures believers that they are saved by grace, through faith, to do good works.

DISCUSSION

Read Ephesians 2:1-10, then answer the following questions.

1. How does Paul describe the contrast between who believers are now compared to who they once were?

2. How is Satan described in verse 2?

3. According to verse 2 and 3, what does it mean to follow the ways of the world?

4. Believers need to know that their former state is the same as every other person. No one is "born" a Christian. Every person on the planet is born with a sinful nature regardless of their parents' faith or lack thereof. We all share the same spiritually dead starting point, period. Ephesians 2:1-4 specifically refers to a dead spiritual state, not a physical state. Therefore, we need to understand that this deadness refers to our spiritual life.

    Why are the ways of the world so attractive?

5. In verses 4-7, what are the present realities of a believer's relationship with Christ?

6. According to verse 5, what does it mean to be made alive in Christ?

7. We are saved by grace not by works. If this is true, then why are good works still important?

8. What must believers do to resist the temptation to follow the ways of the world?

9. It's important to reflect your decision to follow Christ. It reminds us of the new life we have in Christ. What would your life look like today if you had not chosen to become a believer?

FOOD FOR THOUGHT

Paul says the grace of God was manifested by faith. When the time came for God to bring us His grace, He delivered it through faith. It's important to understand what Paul is saying here. Paul has placed these terms in a specific order. Our faith was not the means by which we received grace. Instead, grace was the means by which we received faith.

Paul goes further in Ephesians 2:8 to ensure we do not confuse his point. Paul says "it" (i.e., faith) was not of ourselves. We did not leave our state of spiritual deadness and come to believe God's word by our own efforts. Dead corpses cannot arise themselves. Instead, the faith we received was a gift of God (hence, it was grace). The moment a person is born again and moves from the kingdom of darkness and enters into the light of the truth of the Gospel, they do so because God, by grace, bestowed the gift of faith.

Paul further clarifies that God's manner of salvation precludes any possibility that our newfound state could be attributed to human works. Since our very faith is itself a gift of God, we must acknowledge that we are God's workmanship. Furthermore, God's work presupposes a purpose, and the purpose for His acting is so that we might do good works.

As Jesus Himself said in Matthew 5:16,

"Let our light shine before men in such a way that they may see your good works, and glorify your Father who is in heaven."

Our good works will display the handiwork of God. They do not produce our salvation; they result from our salvation.

Finally, Paul says that even our good works were prepared beforehand by God. When we endeavor to please God by our works, we must accomplish the work He has appointed for us. If we accomplish other work of our own choosing, we labor in our flesh and we do not please the Lord. Therefore, only those works He has purposed beforehand for us constitute good works done in faith.

APPLICATION

Because you were created in Christ to do good works, do a good work this week. Buy coffee for a stranger, help a neighbor, or volunteer to help with a ministry. Demonstrate your faith in some way, shape or form, to others, not because it will save you, but because you are saved.

Describe the word GRACE in your own words:

PRAYER POINTS

- Pray that God will help you to live out your faith.

- Pray that God will reveal where, when and why you need to do a good work to bless someone.

- Pray that God will use you in a significant capacity to help reach someone for Christ and build His church.

STUDY ON YOUR OWN

1. Do a word study on "grace" in the New Testament by reading the passages listed below and write in your own words how grace is depicted:

   Romans 3:21-26

   Titus 3:5

   2 Timothy 1:9

2. Read James 1:22-2:25. In your own words, describe why doing good works is important to you.

3. Memorize Ephesians 2:8-9. To help in memorizing it, write it out several times here:

NOTES

NOTES

THE ROCK THAT RECONCILES
Ephesians 2:11-22

BIBLE READING

- **Sunday:** Ephesians 2:11-22
- **Monday:** Acts 10:34-43
- **Tuesday:** Romans 15:7-13
- **Wednesday:** Matthew 16:13-20
- **Thursday:** Galatians 3:23-29
- **Friday:** 1 Corinthians 12:12-13
- **Saturday:** 2 Corinthians 5:16-19

OPENING DISCUSSION

These are very personal questions, and you might not feel like answering them in the group setting, but they are worth reflecting on.

1. Have you ever been discriminated against for your age, race, gender, or faith? How did it make you feel?

2. Have you, or someone you know, ever looked down on someone else because of their race, age, gender, or economic status? If so, how did God help to change your (or their) perspective?

3. Have you ever helped restore peace between two people? How did it make you feel?

STUDY SUMMARY

Since the Garden of Eden, God's design has been to reconcile all people to Himself. Jesus is the way we all can be reconciled to God. As followers of Christ, we have had His mystery revealed to us. Understanding this helps us to see our continued role in this mystery.

DISCUSSION

Read Ephesians 2:11-22, then answer the following questions.

1. Whenever you see the word "therefore" in the Bible, you should always know what it's there for. In 2:11, what is the "therefore" there for?

2. Ephesians 2:11-12 refers to people groups known as "circumcision" and the "uncircumcision". Who were they?

3. Read 2:14-16. Although this verse is speaking about the unification of the two people groups, it can also refer to joining all people under Christ. Why is this message so important today?

4. What does it mean to be a member of God's household? Why is this important to know?

5. Jesus is referred to as the chief cornerstone in 2:20. Why is it so important to have Christ as the cornerstone of one's faith?

6. According to 2:21-22, believers are joined together to form a holy temple that God indwells with His Spirit. If this is true and believers are all joined together because of Christ, why are there so many different denominations and beliefs?

7. What keeps the church unified? What divides it?

8. How can you help unify the church and keep it focused on its primary purpose?

FOOD FOR THOUGHT

When you sense a friend is in trouble, do you make the first move and call them, or do you sit back and wait for the phone to ring? Do you make the first move and talk to your kids about sex, drugs, and abuse, or wait for them to come to you for advice? When it comes to racial reconciliation, do you wait for someone else to make the first move, or are you willing to walk across racial lines through the tension to meet at the cross?

People know to make the first move when they sense God's leading and take action. They understand the power of the first move and make it at the right time for the right reasons. Making the first move isn't about establishing yourself in a dominant manner; it's about being a catalyst to create positive change in our families and communities.

APPLICATION

This week, seek to be a peacemaker because Jesus is your peace. If you need to ask someone for forgiveness, take a deep breath and reach out to them. If you need to forgive someone, bring the person and the matter before God and trust Him to help you. Reflect on the fact that Jesus is the cornerstone and build your life on His teachings.

Are you willing to make the first move and initiate a conversation? Will you pick up the phone and make the call or walk across the room, hallway, or street to bring peace? Friends, make the first move to show your family, friends, and others what Christian love looks like when it's lived out. Ask for forgiveness, demonstrate grace, show empathy, love others in Jesus' name without judgment or conditions. You can make the first move and be the catalyst to create positive change.

PRAYER POINTS

- Pray for one person around you that you have never really gotten along with or who is much different than you.

- Ask God to help you be a peacemaker.

- Pray that the church will be unified in its mission to make disciples.

STUDY ON YOUR OWN

1. This week, reflect on peacemaking and reconciliation in your own life.

2. In what specific ways can I actively embody the role of a peacemaker in my relationships this week? Are there particular individuals or situations where I feel called to initiate reconciliation or seek forgiveness? Reflect on how Jesus, as your peace, influences your willingness to be the one to go first.

3. Have I been holding onto any grudges or unresolved conflicts with others? How can I bring these issues before God and trust Him to help me forgive and seek reconciliation? Consider how the gospel of peace empowers you to approach these situations with grace and empathy.

4. How does recognizing Jesus as the cornerstone of my life impact the way I respond to conflict and practice forgiveness? Reflect on how grounding your actions and decisions in the teachings of Jesus can transform your approach to making peace and loving others unconditionally.

NOTES

MADE KNOWN
Ephesians 3:1-13

BIBLE READING

- **Sunday:** Ephesians 3:1-13
- **Monday:** Colossians 1:24-27
- **Tuesday:** Romans 16:25-27
- **Wednesday:** 1 Corinthians 2:6-10
- **Thursday:** Acts 26:16-18
- **Friday:** 1 Peter 1:3-12
- **Saturday:** 1 Timothy 1:7-9

OPENING DISCUSSION

1. What's something you enjoy doing that you think could be a contribution to your community or church?

2. Can you think of a time when you tackled a challenge with more confidence than you expected?

STUDY SUMMARY

We all have a job to do. We are a part of a larger community that is God's chosen vehicle (the church) to reveal Himself to our world. We can move ahead boldly, even in the face of harsh opposition, because of our relationship with our creator.

DISCUSSION

Read Ephesians 3:1-13, then answer the following questions.

1. Ephesians 3:7-9 emphasizes that each of us has a unique role in God's plan. What are some ways you've discovered or are discovering your personal role in the church or community? How do you see your strengths and passions contributing to God's mission?

2. How does it feel to think about your life as part of a larger divine plan? What are some practical ways you can align your daily activities or goals with the idea of being part of God's chosen vehicle to reveal Himself to the world?

3. In Ephesians 3:12-13, Paul speaks about approaching God with boldness despite challenges. How do you stay encouraged and confident when facing difficulties in your faith journey? Are there specific practices or reminders that help you maintain boldness?

4. Can you share an experience where you faced opposition or challenges while trying to live out your faith? How did you handle the situation, and what did you learn from it?

5. Ephesians 3:10-11 talks about the church being a key part of God's plan to reveal Himself. How can our church or this group better support each other in fulfilling our roles? What are some ways we can strengthen our community's impact on the world?

6. What are some creative or everyday ways we can reveal God's love to those around us? How can small actions or gestures make a big difference in our communities?

7. How does knowing that God has a plan and that you are a part of it affect your daily decisions and interactions with others? How can this perspective change how we handle everyday situations or long-term goals?

FOOD FOR THOUGHT

"Paul's understanding of the mystery of Christ was not merely an academic or intellectual endeavor; it was a profound revelation that transformed his life and ministry. In Ephesians 3:1-13, Paul highlights the radical inclusiveness of God's grace—the revelation that Gentiles are co-heirs with Israel in the promises of God. This revelation, which was once hidden, underscores the deep unity and peace that Christ brings to all believers. Paul's imprisonment and suffering are not seen as setbacks but as integral parts of God's plan to manifest His manifold wisdom through the church to the world. Thus, the church becomes the living demonstration of God's eternal purpose and grace, showcasing the power of divine reconciliation and unity."

— N.T. Wright[3]

APPLICATION

What is one specific action you can take this week to more actively engage with your role in God's plan? How will you ensure that this action aligns with both your personal gifts and the mission of the church?

PRAYER POINTS

- Pray for insight and empathy for the lost and hurting around you
- Pray for boldness to bring up your faith and share

- Pray for the Spirit's leading in these moments

STUDY ON YOUR OWN

1. How has your understanding of the "mystery" of Christ, as revealed in Ephesians 3:1-13, impacted your view of God's plan for the church and for yourself personally?

2. In light of the passage, what specific role do you feel called to play within your community or church? Consider how you can actively engage in fulfilling this role and contribute to God's mission of revealing His wisdom and grace. What steps can you take this week to align your actions with this calling?

3. Paul talks about enduring suffering and challenges for the sake of the gospel. Reflect on any current difficulties or opposition you are facing in your faith journey. How can the example of Paul's boldness and perseverance encourage you to approach these challenges with a renewed sense of purpose and confidence in God's plan?

NOTES

FULLNESS OF GOD
Ephesians 3:14-21

BIBLE READING

- **Sunday:** Ephesians 3:14-21
- **Monday:** Philippians 1:19-26
- **Tuesday:** Colossians 1:9-14
- **Wednesday:** 2 Corinthians 12:9-10
- **Thursday:** John 17:20-23
- **Friday:** Colossians 2:6-15
- **Saturday:** Psalm 16

OPENING DISCUSSION

1. What is your favorite love story? Why?

2. Why do you think love is important to us as human beings?

3. What are some ways you like to give/receive love?

STUDY SUMMARY

We all want to be loved. We all want to be accepted. It is built into us from birth. Jesus fills that need in our lives. As we begin to live His way, it can be difficult. The Apostle Paul earnestly prayed that we would continue to rely on the power of the Holy Spirit, who is at work in our lives (Ephesian 3:14-17a).

In Christ, we can experience a love that surpasses anything this world can offer (Ephesians 3:17b-19). That love compels us forward into the work God has for us. That love compels us forward into a life postured towards God in worship (Ephesians 3:20-21).

DISCUSSION

Read Ephesians 3:14-21, then answer the following questions.

1. What is the reason Paul kneels before the Father?

2. What do you think it means that every family derives its name from the Father?

3. Paul makes several pleas or prayers for his readers. According to 3:16-17a, what is Paul's first prayer for his readers? Where will this request be fulfilled from? For what purpose is this request made?

4. How are we strengthened by the Holy Spirit? What does that look like in our lives today?

5. A second plea or prayer begins in 3:17b. What does it mean to be rooted and established in love?

6. Looking at 3:18, what is Paul's plea for his readers? What is the result of this request?

7. What does rooted and established in the love of Christ look like in our lives today?

8. What is Paul's response (found in 3:20-21) to the reality that the fullness of God is found in us through the love of Christ and the power of the Holy Spirit at work in us?

9. What is your reaction to the reality that the fullness of God is found in you through the love of Christ and the power of the Holy Spirit at work in you?

FOOD FOR THOUGHT

"Love is not peripheral, love is not extraneous, love is not something on the circumference, love is not a hit and miss, now and then, love is not a minor detail, it is the essential root and ground of all that you are. When Christ dominates your life, the characteristic will be love. You will love in the way that He loved. The very love by which God is known, for God is love, by which God is manifest, for Jesus Christ is love manifest, will flow through you."

-John F. MacArthur[4]

APPLICATION

This week, live in this reality: the love of Christ has no limits. Its impact in your life is far reaching. Know that you are loved. Ask God to show you how loved you are. Let your actions flow out of His love for you. If you don't know the love God has for you, God's love will not show in your actions. So, seek out an understanding of His love for you and let it show in your life.

PRAYER POINTS

- Pray for a greater realization of the power of the Holy Spirit in you.

- Pray for a deepening of the love of Christ in your life, seen in your actions.

- Praise the LORD for what He has done in you!

STUDY ON YOUR OWN

1. Read Colossians 2:6-7. What does it look like to live your life in Christ? How is your faith strengthened?

2. Read John 15:9-17. What does this passage say about love? What does the love Christ has for us look like? What does the same love in us look like?

3. Memorize Ephesians 3:20-21. To help in memorizing it, write it out several times here:

NOTES

BE ONE TO BRING LIFE
Ephesians 4:1-16

BIBLE READING

- **Sunday:** Ephesians 4:1-16
- **Monday:** 1 Corinthians 12:4-11
- **Tuesday:** Romans 12:1-8
- **Wednesday:** Colossians 3:16-17
- **Thursday:** 1 Peter 4:10-11
- **Friday:** 1 Timothy 4:11-16
- **Saturday:** Acts 6:1-7

OPENING DISCUSSION

1. Share a time when you tried to do something by yourself when you should have asked for someone to help you. Why didn't you ask for help?

2. What first attracted you to the church?

STUDY SUMMARY

In Christ, there is a high calling on our lives. We are not to live in the same manner as the world around us (Ephesians 4:1-3). This can be difficult to do on your own. That is why God's intended purpose is for us to be united in Him. We are to be united by our faith (Ephesians 4:4-6). In unity we each have our own job to do and have been given a unique skill set to accomplish our God-given job (Ephesians 4:7-13).

DISCUSSION

Read Ephesians 4:1-16, then answer the following questions.

1. According to verse 1, every believer has a calling. What is your calling? Has it changed? Are you serving in that area?

2. Do you see areas of your life that do not line up to the high calling God has placed on your life?

3. According to 4:3, you are called to protect unity in this body (the church). Believers should have a disposition toward unity so that their responses to difficult conversations, disagreements or situations are governed by their higher calling to love others through the bond of peace. There is great wisdom to be found here. The Holy Spirit is showing the church how to maintain community. Why is it so important for a body of believers to be united in peace?

4. Think about Christ's gift of peace. What difference does this gift make for you when you are facing stresses or conflicts? Refer to verse 3.

5. What kinds of things have you observed that tend to sabotage Christ's peace among believers?

6. Are there any effective ways of preventing or addressing these peace-stealing attitudes or actions?

7. What might you do to strengthen the "bond of peace" in your group, church, or peers?

8. Paul says we have one body, one Spirit, one hope, one Lord, one faith, one baptism and one God and Father of all (verses 4-6). How do these seven "ones" contribute to actually living out true unity?

9. Where does the notion that you can grow in your faith without community come from? Is this biblical? Refer to verse 16.

FOOD FOR THOUGHT

"In Ephesians 4:1-16, Paul calls the church to live out the unity of the Spirit in the bond of peace, stressing the importance of maintaining unity amidst diversity. The church is portrayed as a body with Christ as the head, where every member has a role and function. The diverse gifts given to individuals are meant to build up the body, achieving maturity and fullness in Christ. This passage highlights that Christian maturity involves not only a personal transformation but also a commitment to relational harmony and collective growth. The goal is not simply personal holiness but the corporate development of the body of Christ, reflecting His love and grace in every aspect of communal life."

— John Stott[5]

APPLICATION

In verse 16, Paul says that the body "grows and builds itself up in love, as each part does its work." What steps must you take to more fully work toward this goal? This week, list one action you plan to take to bring unity to the body.

PRAYER POINTS

- Pray that your spiritual gifts will be used to help others grow in Christ and to build the church.

- If you need to make peace with someone, pray about taking a step forward this week.

STUDY ON YOUR OWN

1. In Ephesians 4:8-10, Christ is compared to a conquering hero whose victory parade fills "the whole universe." From the highest heaven to the lowest earth. Then, Jesus generously distributes spiritual gifts to His faithful followers. According to verses 11-13; what is the nature and purpose of these gifts?

2. Explain how spiritual infancy differs from spiritual maturity. Refer to verses 14-16.

3. What spiritual gifts do you think you might have? Refer to 1 Corinthians 12 for a partial list of spiritual gifts.

4. How do these spiritual gifts fulfill the purposes described in verses 11-13?

5. Count how many times the word "unity" or "one" is used in Ephesians 4:1-16. Write down how it is being used in each case.

NOTES

PUT ON THE NEW SELF
Ephesians 4:17-32

BIBLE READING

- **Sunday:** Ephesians 4:17-32
- **Monday:** Colossians 3:5-14
- **Tuesday:** Romans 6:1-14
- **Wednesday:** Galatians 5:16-26
- **Thursday:** 1 John 1:5-10
- **Friday:** James 1:21-25
- **Saturday:** 2 Corinthians 5:17-21; Galatians 2:20

OPENING DISCUSSION

In terms of how you live and your daily behavior, what are the biggest ways you are different now in Christ from what you were before Christ?

STUDY SUMMARY

This week we are contrasting the old and new ways of living for believers. In Ephesians 4:17-32, Paul urges Christians to abandon their former, corrupt lifestyles characterized by ignorance, impurity, and deceit. Instead, they are called to embrace a new way of life that reflects their renewed nature in Christ. This involves putting off the old self and adopting a new self, created to be righteous and holy. Paul emphasizes practical behaviors of the new life, including honesty, controlled anger, productive work, and kind, forgiving interactions with others. The passage underscores the importance of living in a manner consistent with one's identity in Christ, marked by truth, righteousness, and love.

DISCUSSION

Read Ephesians 4:17-32, then answer the following questions.

1. Unbelievers harden their own hearts when they ignore God and suppress their own conscience until it is seared (1 Timothy 4:2). What is the result?

2. According to Romans 1:18-22, what else do unbelievers suppress when they choose to ignore God? What do they become (verse 22)?

3. According to Ephesians 4:19, when unbelievers' hearts become more and more callous, what kinds of things dominate their thoughts and eventually their actions (verse 19)?

4. Believers also have an "old nature", (also called our sin nature or the flesh) that is just as corrupt as an unbeliever's. This is why believers can sometimes think and act just as bad as the worst pagan. How do believers overcome their sin nature?

Read again Ephesians 4:20-24.

5. "Putting off" and "putting on" refers to what we do with clothing. Putting off is an image of separation from dirty clothing. What might this separating from your old nature look like? How often does a person typically change clothes?

6. According to verse 22, what is happening to our old nature? What insights does that give you for dealing with sin in your life?

7. Can you think of any ways your new nature is growing stronger?

8. Read Ephesians 4:25-32. Paul gives five specific exhortations to "put off old behavior" and "put on new", followed by a reason why. Fill in the chart below.

	DON'T!	DO.	WHY?
Verse 25			
Verses 26-27			
Verse 28			
Verse 29			
Verses 31-32			

FOOD FOR THOUGHT

"In Ephesians 4:17-32, Paul describes the transformation expected in the lives of believers. The old self, which is marked by deceit and corruption, must be left behind. Instead, believers are called to live out their new identity in Christ, characterized by righteousness and holiness. This involves practical changes in behavior, such as speaking the truth, managing anger, and showing kindness and forgiveness. Paul's teaching underscores that the Christian life is not merely about avoiding sin but actively embodying a new way of living that reflects our renewed nature and relationships in Christ."

— Tim Chester[6]

"Do not be overcome by evil, but overcome evil with good."

-Romans 12:21

APPLICATION

This week, let's focus on making practical changes in our daily lives as we strive to align with the new self Paul describes in Ephesians 4:17-32. Reflect on areas where old habits, such as deceit, impurity, or uncontrolled anger, may still influence you. Take deliberate steps to put off these old behaviors and embrace the new way of living that Christ calls us to. This means practicing honesty in your interactions, managing anger constructively, engaging in work that is both productive and ethical, and extending kindness and forgiveness to others. As you go about your week, ask yourself how you can embody the truth, righteousness, and love that reflect your renewed identity in Christ. By consciously choosing behaviors that align with your new nature, you will better demonstrate the transformative power of the gospel in your everyday life.

PRAYER POINTS

- Can you select one specific "put on" and one "put off" to ask the Holy Spirit to give you supernatural power to accomplish this week? Write them here:

  Put on: _____

  Put off: _____

- Ask the Holy Spirit to reveal anything in your life that might be grieving Him.

- Ask God to give you wisdom to speak a word of encouragement to your spouse, your family members, friends, and coworkers this week.

STUDY ON YOUR OWN

1. What are some specific areas in my life where old habits or patterns of behavior (such as deceit, impurity, or uncontrolled anger) still influence me? What steps can I take to consciously "put off" these old behaviors?

   Colossians 3:8-10

   Romans 13:12-14

2. How can I actively practice the new behaviors Paul describes, such as honesty, controlled anger, productive work, and kindness? Identify practical ways to incorporate these virtues into my daily life and interactions.

3. In what ways can I better reflect my identity in Christ through my actions and attitudes? How does understanding my new identity in Christ affect how I approach conflicts, work, and relationships?

Galatians 2:20

1 Peter 2:9

Philippians 2:14-15

NOTES

NOTES

EMPOWERED CHILDREN OF LIGHT
Ephesians 5:1-20

BIBLE READING

- **Sunday:** Ephesians 5:1-20
- **Monday:** Philippians 2:1-11
- **Tuesday:** Colossians 3:15-17
- **Wednesday:** 1 John 3:1-10
- **Thursday:** Matthew 5:13-16
- **Friday:** Romans 12:1-2
- **Saturday:** 2 Timothy 1:7-9

OPENING DISCUSSION

1. Christians are called to live differently from the society around them. How do you live differently from unbelievers around you?

2. What do you think it means to be filled with the Spirit? Why is it important?

3. In this week's passage from Ephesians, Paul urges believers to be filled with the Holy Spirit. How do you think believers are filled with the Holy Spirit?

STUDY SUMMARY

Believers should live as children of the light with renewed thoughts and attitudes, resulting in different behaviors. So how do believers stop telling lies, control their anger, be scrupulously honest, refrain from foul and abusive language, and abstain from sexual immorality? How do they replace negative behaviors with generosity, kindness, mercy, and forgiveness? It's supernatural.

But the mystery has already been revealed to believers who are empowered by the Holy Spirit of God. The filling of the Holy Spirit must be appropriated by faith as we surrender our lives to the Lordship of Jesus.

DISCUSSION

Read Ephesians 5:1-20, then answer the following questions.

1. According to Ephesians 5:1-2, as dearly loved children, believers are to imitate their Father and show self-sacrificing love to others. What could you sacrifice (give up) for the benefit of another this week?

2. Read Ephesians 5:3. God is all for sex in marriage; He created it! But the admonition against "sexual immorality," (Greek *porneia* from which we get the word pornography) means sexual activity outside of marriage. According to 1 Corinthians 6:18, *porneia* is harmful. Why is it harmful? What practical steps can you take this week to protect yourself from these pervasive temptations?

3. Practically and with wisdom, how should you respond when confronted with obscenities and coarse joking? Consider the last phrase of Ephesians 5:4.

4. Read John 14:16-17, Romans 8:9 and Ephesians 1:13. What does the scripture teach about the Holy Spirit indwelling believers?

5. Are you indwelt by the Holy Spirit? Do you ever doubt it? Why or why not?

6. What are some evidences of the indwelling Holy Spirit according to the following verses? John 16:7-8, 13, Romans 5:5, 1 Corinthians 2:12-15.

7. According to Galatians 3:2-5, how did believers receive the Holy Spirit (verse 2)? How does God continue to provide believers with the Spirit's power (verse 5)?

8. Read Colossians 3:16. In this parallel passage, what are believers to fill their minds with? How can you accomplish that in your life?

9. If sin grieves the Holy Spirit (Ephesians 4:30), how can believers reconnect with God and once again become filled with His Spirit?

10. Read 1 John 1:9

FOOD FOR THOUGHT

"Ephesians 5:1-20 challenges us to live as 'children of light,' which is only possible through being filled with the Holy Spirit. This passage reveals that a Spirit-filled life is characterized by a deep, joyful relationship with God, expressed through worship, gratitude, and righteous living. The Holy Spirit empowers believers to reflect Christ's love and purity in all areas of life, transforming everyday actions into acts of worship. As we seek to be continually filled with the Spirit, our lives will increasingly exhibit the light of Christ, guiding us away from the darkness of our former selves and into the vibrant, transformative life that God intends for us."

— Bryan Chapell[7]

APPLICATION

All Christians are indwelt by the Holy Spirit, but not all are filled by the Holy Spirit.

In Ephesians 5:1-20, Paul calls believers to live as children of light, characterized by love, purity, and wisdom. Central to this passage is the imperative to be filled with the Holy Spirit, which is vital for embodying these qualities. To apply this, intentionally seek the Holy Spirit's guidance in your daily life through prayer, worship, and reading Scripture. Ask the Spirit to fill you with His presence and to transform your actions and attitudes. This means allowing the Spirit to influence your decisions, interactions, and overall approach to life. Cultivate a heart of gratitude and joy, as these are marks of a Spirit-filled life, and let your conduct reflect the new identity you have in Christ. As you are empowered by the Spirit, you will naturally exhibit love, make wise choices, and live out a faith that glorifies God and impacts those around you.

PRAYER POINTS

- Spend time in confession to God for the ongoing sin in your life

- Ask the Holy Spirit for the strength to live as a child of light

- Invite the Holy Spirit to continue to make you new and lead you daily

STUDY ON YOUR OWN

1. In Galatians 5, Paul likens being controlled by the Spirit to "living in", "walking in step with", and being "led" by the Holy Spirit (Galatians 5:16-18). What are the results of being controlled by the Holy Spirit? (Galatians 5:22-23)

2. According to John 16:13, and Acts 1:8 & 2:4, what are some other results of being filled with the Holy Spirit?

3. According to Acts 9:31 and John 14:26, how does the Holy Spirit minister to those who are hurting?

4. How can you understand what God's will is? (John 8:31-32, John 16:12-14)

NOTES

MOST HATED WORD
Ephesians 5:21-33

BIBLE READING

- **Sunday:** Ephesians 5:21-33
- **Monday:** James 4:1-10
- **Tuesday:** 1 Peter 5:5-6
- **Wednesday:** Genesis 2:18-25)
- **Thursday:** 1 Corinthians 7:1-16
- **Friday:** Proverbs 31:10-31
- **Saturday:** Titus 3:1-8

OPENING DISCUSSION

1. Who was the authority figure in your home growing up? Do you have good memories of this person or bad ones?

2. How has the primary authority figure in your formative years impacted the way you view authority today? How well do you work with authority?

3. When you hear the word "submit" what feeling does it evoke? Are they positive, neutral, negative, or difficult to put into words?

STUDY SUMMARY

Relationships can be hard. Often, it is the relationships with those closest to us that are the most difficult and can bring the most damage. They also can bring the most impact for Christ when done his way, which is characterized by humility and submission to Christ in our marriage (Ephesians 5:22-33), in our parenting (Ephesians 6:1-4), and in our workplace (Ephesians 6:5-9).

DISCUSSION

Read Ephesians 5:21-33, then answer the following questions.

1. What is required before a person can make his or her marriage and family what God intends them to be? Explain.

2. If you are married, do you consider your marriage to be based on an authoritarian model, equalitarian model, or complementarian model?

    - **Authoritarian Model:** In this model, one partner (typically the husband in traditional contexts) holds primary authority and makes most of the decisions within the marriage. The other partner is expected to submit to this authority. This model emphasizes a hierarchical structure where power and decision-making are concentrated in one person, often leading to a dynamic where one partner's needs and desires are prioritized over the other's.

    - **Equalitarian Model:** The equalitarian model advocates for equal partnership in marriage, where both spouses share authority, responsibilities, and decision-making equally. In this model, there is no hierarchical structure; instead, both partners collaborate and contribute equally to the marriage. Decisions are made jointly, and both partners' needs and perspectives are considered equally important.

    - **Complementarian Model:** The complementarian model acknowledges distinct roles for each partner in a marriage, with the belief that these roles complement each other to create a harmonious relationship. While it maintains that the husband often has a leadership role and the wife supports this leadership, it also emphasizes mutual respect, support, and love. Each partner contributes differently but in a way that is believed to enhance the marriage and reflect their complementary strengths.

3. The idea of "submission" in the biblical marital context is this: "to put oneself beneath another in recognition of God's sovereignty and goodness." Does this mean a wife should submit to her husband in everything? Explain.

    Describe a scenario when "submitting" is the wrong thing to do.

4. What does it mean for a man to "love your wife as Christ loves the church?"

5. How can understanding Christ's sacrificial love for the church help us apply this concept in practical ways within our own marriages? Can you identify specific actions or attitudes that embody this kind of love in everyday life?

6. Verse 33 refers to the concept of "love and respect." The "love and respect" concept is this: More than anything, women want to be loved and men want to be respected. Do you think this is true?

7. In what ways can understanding the differing needs for love and respect between spouses enhance communication and resolve conflicts in marriage? Can you share any personal experiences or observations that illustrate how addressing these needs has impacted a relationship?

8. How can couples practically show love and respect to each other in ways that align with their individual needs? Are there specific strategies or practices you think are effective for ensuring that both partners feel valued and understood?

FOOD FOR THOUGHT

"Ephesians 5:21-33 presents a vision of marriage that is profoundly counter-cultural. Paul calls for a relationship where love and respect are not only given but are essential to the partnership. Husbands are to love their wives with a sacrificial love, emulating Christ's love for the church, which is self-giving and nurturing. Wives are to respect their husbands, which is not merely a cultural expectation but a reflection of a deeper, mutual submission that reflects the unity of Christ and the church. This passage challenges us to live out a marriage characterized by mutual honor and sacrificial love, which in turn serves as a living testimony of Christ's relationship with His people. It's about embodying a radical and transformative love that goes beyond conventional expectations, shaping our marriages to reflect the gospel in a profound way."

— Tim Keller[8]

APPLICATION

If you are married, this section of text should impact how you treat one another. It is essential that believers develop a proper understanding of what it means to "submit to one another out of reverence for Christ." Once we understand what this means, it should be expressed within the family unit. Submitting to one another out of reverence for Christ actually creates unity, demonstrates love, and models a Christ-like attitude.

This week, couples should lean into the concept of submitting to one another out of reverence for Christ, because it will help you and your spouse grow closer together. Don't wait for someone else to take the first step, you do it.

PRAYER POINTS

- If you are married, ask God to strengthen your marriage by helping you and your spouse to submit to one another out of reverence for Christ. Pray for your spouse by name everyday this week.

- Pray that God will soften your heart towards someone in authority that has abused it in the past. Ask God to soften your heart not to give a free pass to that person, but so that you can be free from that person.

STUDY ON YOUR OWN

1. How does a person submit to an authority or others without becoming a doormat? When is it right to say "no"?

2. If you are married, what is the one take-away that you will keep in mind about your role in the husband/wife relationship?

3. Paul writes "let us therefore make every effort to do what leads to peace and to mutual edification" (Romans 14:19). How will you begin to practice this verse in your marriage?

4. Has your understanding of the concept of submission and love in a marriage been changed during this study? If so, how?

NOTES

NOTES

SECOND MOST HATED WORD

Ephesians 6:1-9

BIBLE READING

- **Sunday:** Ephesians 6:1-9
- **Monday:** Colossians 3:20-25
- **Tuesday:** Psalm 1
- **Wednesday:** 1 Peter 2:18-25
- **Thursday:** Romans 6:15-23
- **Friday:** Titus 2:1-10
- **Saturday:** James 4:6-10

OPENING DISCUSSION

1. Describe your worst boss ever (don't use names). What made them such a bad boss? How did that impact your work?

2. When you hear the word "obey" what feeling does it evoke? Are they positive, neutral, negative, or difficult to put into words?

STUDY SUMMARY

In Ephesians 6:1-9, Paul provides practical guidance on living out the Christian faith within the family and workplace. He emphasizes the importance of obedience, both for children towards their parents and for servants (or employees) towards their masters (or employers). Children are instructed to honor and obey their parents as a reflection of their commitment to the Lord, promising blessings and long life as a result. Similarly, Paul calls on servants to work diligently and sincerely, as if serving Christ rather than men, highlighting that their work is ultimately for God. Masters are also urged to treat their servants with fairness and respect, recognizing that they, too, are accountable to God. This passage underscores that true obedience stems from a heart devoted to Christ, impacting every aspect of life, from family dynamics to professional conduct. By aligning their actions with God's will, believers demonstrate their faith through their relationships and responsibilities.

DISCUSSION

Read Ephesians 6:1-9, then answer the following questions.

1. Why is it hard for some (of course not yourself) to obey authority figures over them?

2. What makes it easier to obey authority?

3. There are three primary parenting styles, Authoritarian, Permissive, and Authoritative.

    Authoritarian parenting involves more dictating and little listening.

    Permissive parents let their kids do whatever they want.

    Authoritative parents want to lead and guide their children by providing boundaries and encouragement.

    Read Proverbs 22:6 and Ephesians 5:4. What style of parenting do these verses teach? Does your style line up with scripture?

4. If you remove the word "slave" in 6:5-8 and think of it in terms of your work environment, what principles apply?

5. If you own a business or supervise others, how does 6:9 apply to you?

6. If you manage others—or if you were to become a manager tomorrow—how can you glorify God in the way you treat your employees?

   - How would you handle conflict differently than a non Christian manager?

   - How would you handle underperforming employees differently?

FOOD FOR THOUGHT

"In Ephesians 6:1-9, Paul addresses the dynamic of obedience within the family and workplace, framing it as an expression of our relationship with God. He emphasizes that children are called to obey their parents not simply out of duty but as an act of reverence for Christ, and similarly, servants are to work wholeheartedly, knowing that their true Master is in heaven. This perspective transforms everyday tasks and relationships into opportunities for spiritual growth and witness. Paul's instructions remind us that the quality of our obedience in the mundane aspects of life reflects our deeper commitment to Christ. It's a call to integrate faith with practice, ensuring that every act of obedience is infused with sincerity and reverence for God."

— John Stott[9]

APPLICATION

If you have children, treat them with love and respect. Don't exasperate them by constantly pointing out their faults. It's okay to correct and coach them when needed, but at the end of the day you need to model love and grace. Praise them for what they do right and guide them with God's Word trusting the Holy Spirit to work in their life.

And if you are still living under your parent's authority, focus on honoring Christ by honoring your parents. If you are living in a single parent family, have a stepparent, or traditional family structure, the same principles apply. Your parents will make mistakes and you may disagree with their decisions at times, but ultimately, they are responsible to help guide you until you are on your own. The best thing you can do is practice honest and open conversation with your parents.

In your workplace, honor Christ by being an honest, hard working employee - even if your boss is terrible. And likewise, if you have authority over others, manage them well, knowing it is a reflection of Christ to them.

PRAYER POINTS

- If you have children, pray for them by name every day this week. Thank God for three positive qualities they have every time you pray.

- If you have a boss, pray for them by name every day this week. Thank God for three positive qualities they have every time you pray.

- If you have employees, pray for them by name every day this week. Thank God for three positive qualities they have every time you pray.

STUDY ON YOUR OWN

1. How can viewing your responsibilities at home or work as acts of reverence for Christ change the way you approach them? Reflect on specific tasks or interactions where you might apply this perspective to deepen your commitment and sincerity.

2. Our obedience reflects our commitment to Christ.

   In what areas of your life—whether in relationships with family or in your professional environment—could you improve in demonstrating wholeheartedness and integrity? How might this shift impact your daily life and relationships?

3. Consider a recent situation where you struggled with obedience or responsibility. How can Paul's instructions and the idea of seeing Christ as your ultimate Master help you address and overcome these challenges? What practical steps can you take to align your actions more closely with your faith?

NOTES

MAKE WAR
Ephesians 6:10-24

BIBLE READING

- **Sunday:** Ephesians 6:10-24
- **Monday:** 2 Corinthians 10:3-5
- **Tuesday:** Romans 12:1-2
- **Wednesday:** 1 Peter 5:6-11
- **Thursday:** Revelation 12:7-12
- **Friday:** Matthew 4:1-11
- **Saturday:** 1 John 5:4-5

OPENING DISCUSSION

1. Hollywood loves to give us action movies. Action movies are often filled with fight sequences. What makes a good fight scene? Why do you think we, as Americans, are drawn to these types of movies?

2. If you were called to fight in a battle right now and could only grab 3 things from your house, what would they be and why?

STUDY SUMMARY

Living for God is not easy. Often it is the more difficult path in this life. Living in contrast to the majority culture around us means we have to continually be seeking Jesus. Thankfully, God has given us the tools to defend ourselves from the enemy's attempts to discount our message and discourage our pursuit of Christ. With these tools put to use in our life, we can stand strong in the Lord, shining His light in the darkness around us.

DISCUSSION

Read Ephesians 6:10-24, then answer the following questions.

1. What does it mean to "be strong in the Lord"?

2. In 6:11-17, compare the commands to "Put on," "Take your stand," "stand firm," "take," and "take up." How many times are these words used? What are the similarities and differences in these commands?

3. Who is our fight against?

4. Why is it so important to put on the armor of God?

5. What are the armor of God?

6. What does it look like to be equipped with the belt of truth?

7. What does it look like to be equipped with the breastplate of righteousness?

8. What does it look like to have feet fitted with the gospel of peace?

9. What does it look like to wield the shield of faith and helmet of salvation?

10. What does it look like to possess the sword of the spirit?

11. According to verses 18-20, what can we continually do in this fight? Why is this so vital to this fight?

FOOD FOR THOUGHT

"The battle isn't against other people, though they may be involved. The battle is a spiritual one, and the battlefield keeps changing. We are called to fight the "good fight." You will discover that the struggle may be about finances, marriage, or employment - but no matter where you are called to battle - keep fighting. Don't give up!"

-James MacDonald[10]

APPLICATION

The Armor of God is essential for spiritual warfare. We need to be to be prepared and protected against spiritual challenges. Applying this passage involves actively putting on each piece of armor daily: the belt of truth, which grounds us in the reality of God's Word; the breastplate of righteousness, which guards our hearts from the accusations and temptations of the enemy; the readiness of the gospel of peace, which equips us to face conflict with a foundation of reconciliation and hope; the shield of faith, which extinguishes the fiery darts of doubt and fear; the helmet of salvation, which secures our minds with the assurance of Christ's redemptive work; and the sword of the Spirit, which is the Word of God, used for both defense and offense in spiritual battles.

By consciously embracing these elements, we align ourselves with God's strength and protection, enabling us to stand firm in our faith amidst life's trials. This daily practice not only fortifies us personally but also prepares us to effectively engage in the broader mission of advancing God's kingdom.

Put on the armor. Make War.

PRAYER POINTS

- Pray for those that are investing in you spiritually (mentors/pastors/etc.). Pray that God would keep them faithful in their mission and calling.

- Pray for fellow believers who are facing various struggles and persecutions around the world.

- Pray that you would continue to stand with the armor of God protecting you in the midst of attacks from the evil one.

STUDY ON YOUR OWN

1. Read the following passages to do a Word Study on truth and righteousness in the New Testament. Focus on how to understand these spiritual realities and how they protect us as elements of the armor of God.

   a. **Truth**

   - John 14:6

- John 17:17

- Ephesians 6:14

- 1 John 1:6

- 1 John 3:18

b. **Righteousness**

  - Matthew 5:6

  - Romans 3:22

  - Romans 14:17

  - Philippians 3:9

  - 2 Timothy 2:22

2. Equipping ourselves with God's armor means we must face realities of sin in our lives. Look at Hebrews 12:4-13. What does this teach us about God's discipline? How is discipline beneficial for us?

- Where might you need to confess sin and follow God's discipline in your own life?

3. Memorize Ephesians 6:10-17. It's long, but you can do it!

NOTES

ENDNOTES

[1] McGee, J. Vernon. *Thru the Bible with J. Vernon McGee*. Thomas Nelson, 1983.

[2, 8] Keller, Timothy. *The Meaning of Marriage: Facing the Complexities of Commitment with the Wisdom of God*. Penguin Books, 2011.

[3] Wright, N. T. *Paul for Everyone: The Prison Letters. Society for Promoting Christian Knowledge*, 2004.

[4] MacArthur, John F. *The Love of God: A Season of Hope*. HarperOne, 2009.

[5, 9] Stott, John. *The Message of Ephesians: God's New Society*. InterVarsity Press, 1979.

[6] Chester, Tim. *Ephesians for You*. The Good Book Company, 2013.

[7] Chapell, Bryan. *Ephesians: The Gospel of God's Grace*. Crossway, 2011.

[10] MacDonald, James. *When Life Is Hard*. Moody Publishers, 2011.

WATCH

View the messages in the Ephesians series and more by scanning the QR code below or visiting

www.freshwater.church/weekly-messages

EVENTS

PODCAST

FAITH
STORIES

Learn more at
freshwater.church

Made in the USA
Columbia, SC
10 September 2024

41489841R00052